THE
Archive Photographs
SERIES

OSWESTRY

Aerial view of Oswestry showing the Gobowen line with the Railway works in the foreground.

Cover photograph: Rabbits and damsons for sale at Lloyds (photographer and taxidermist) of Willow Street.

THE Archive Photographs SERIES
OSWESTRY

Compiled by
Bernard Mitchell

THE
CHALFORD
PRESS

BATH • AUGUSTA • RENNES

The Chalford Publishing Company Limited
St Mary's Mill
Chalford
Stroud
Gloucestershire
GL6 8NX

ISBN 0 7524 0032 0

Printed in Great Britain by
Redwood Books, Trowbridge, Wiltshire

Llwyd Mansion, built by John Lloyd or Llwyd of Llanforda. Pictured here after its restoration in 1875.

Contents

Acknowledgements   6

Introduction   7

1.   Oswestry Town   9

2.   Industry and Transport   57

3.   The Outskirts   77

4.   Sport   93

5.   The 1950s and 1960s   101

The Bailey Head market during the 1950s. Note the signpost A483 to Wrexham on Albion Hill.

Acknowledgements

I would like to thank all those people who have kindly supplied photographs and information for this book. I am particularly grateful to the editor and readers of the *Border Counties Advertizer*; Mr John Strange and to my wife, Anne, for her help in the darkroom and with the preparation of the book. I thank you all.

Introduction

The market town of Oswestry lies on the border between England and Wales. It is a town which, for over 800 years, has developed a unique character with a combination of Celtic and Saxon peoples.

The streets of the centre of the town have the same pattern now as they have had for hundreds of years. However, the development of the town from its early days as a trading centre between the Welsh hill farmers and the people of the Shropshire plains has been affected by the introduction of new industries, both within Oswestry and on its periphery.

The town's role as a rail centre after the Cambrian Railway made its headquarters here in the 1860s, the coal mines at Ifton and Trefonen and the draughting of thousands of troops to Park Hall Camp during two world wars, as well as the setting up of the Robert Jones and Agnes Hunt Orthopaedic Hospital, all added to the further development of the town as a thriving industrial and commercial centre.

I have, in the book, endeavoured to show in photographs the development of Oswestry from a market town through the expanding industrial and railway period of the Victorian era to the decline of those indusrtries in the 1960s.

A traveller passing through Oswestry around the turn of the century wrote:

Modern Oswestry is a place of engineering shops, foundries and mining interests, and, as the seat of the Cambrian Railway locomotive and carriage works, is busy and prosperous. Not a vestige of its old trade in Welsh flannel remains, for the mills of Lancashire long ago began to produce a cheaper article than the Welsh could make. Very little of the old Oswestry is left, and although the streets are for the most part narrow and crooked, the greater number of the houses are modern. Inns abound in the grimy and slovenly place; a very different state of things from a hundred years ago, when Rowlandson and Wigstead came here and found it remarkable for having (though rather large a town) the fewest public-houses we ever witnessed. No one is likely to raise that complaint in these times.
(*The Holyhead Road* by Charles Harper 1902)

As with all living things, the spirit of the town is constantly changing. It is the people as much as the architecture that create the nature of Oswestry as we know it. The changing fashions, the social and business activities are all relevant to the historical evolution of the town, as reflected in a recent poem:

Moving On

How much we have lost
Can we tell what is gone
As we strive to make progress
We seldom think of our loss

The Cambrian sidings lie in rust
The station put to sleep
Steam engines have ceased their throng
The line now turned to green

Llwyd Mansion is standing strong
Though many trades have come and gone
The landscape may be different now
But the farmer carries on

We have progressed in this little town
Where apathy is strong
On the way we have lost some roots
But the growing carries on.

(E.J.M. 1994)

A general view of the railway sidings.

One
Oswestry Town

A 1950s photograph of Church Street facing the Cross.

Church Street from the Cross.

The Cross.

10

Church Street with the Wynnstay Hotel and the Oak Inn, first recorded in 1792.

Church Street showing the Post Office which closed in 1962 and the original Lloyd's Bank.

The magnificent shop front of James Baker at 23 the Cross.

Staff at R. Jones & Sons of Salop Road.

Mrs Griffiths the wife of W. Griffiths, corn and seed merchant of Bailey Street which is now part of the George Hotel.

An early Victorian photograph of the stone cross and pump *in situ* at the cross. It was a market cross erected in 1862 and can now be seen at Castle Bank.

A busy scene at the Cross. The People's Boot Mart is on the left.

The Cross, Oswestry.

Bargain hunting at the Cross Market which was built in 1842.

New Street viewed across the rubble of the Old Cross Market Hall with Tesco's store in the background.

Regulars at the White Horse Hotel, Church Street. The horse on the sign lost its leg during the riot after the election of 1832.

The skittle bowlers team at the Cross Keys Inn, Cross Street.

The Butcher's Arms, Willow Street, showing the entry to Arthur Street (The Butcher's Arms Shut). In 1691 the inn became the meeting place of the Independent Church, forerunner of Christchurch United Reformed Church.

A fine display of ironmongery at Lacon's of Leg Street who began trading there in 1786.

Twin-tubs and wringers at the new Electricity Board showrooms in Salop Road, 1960.

Snow covers the Central car park—formerly the Smithfield—with the Kwik Save supermarket before redevelopment.

Construction in progress at the new Post Office in Willow Street, which was built by W. Watkin & Co.

Arthur Street looking towards the Butcher's Arms Shut with cottages on the left , now demolished.

Staff at Oswestry's last working abattoir at the rear of Welsh Walls.

J. Boffey, butchers, of the Quadrant, Leg Street. The building is recorded as having been used for this purpose since 1862. It is now Eric Roberts & Sons.

A fine display of meat outside J. Faulks & Sons of Leg Street, formerly of Rutland, 1860.

The Victoria Garage, now Beauclerk's.

The inner courtyard of Victoria Garage (now Beauclerks), Victoria Road. It was formerly a foundry.

David Davies & Sons workers outside their premises in Upper Church Street, *c.* 1910.

Staff of David Davies & Sons lead a funeral procession along Victoria Road to Oswestry cemetery.

23

The Bell Inn, Church Street, first mentioned in 1663. Prisoners were billeted here during the Napoleonic wars.

A warm welcome for the Shropshire Imperial Yeomanry from the staff of the Greyhound Inn, Willow Street.

The Crown Inn, Beatrice Street.

The Grapes Hotel, formerly known as the
Little Cross Keys, dating back in parish
records to 1688. It is now Gibsons.

A Round Table Christmas parade in Church Street.

Shop assistants from Oswestry Cooperative Society shop, whose float won first prize in the 1938 carnival.

The carnival procession passes along Oswald Road, *c.* 1950.

Kitchen staff at the National School, Welsh Walls, which is now the Walls Restaurant..

Pupils at the National School, Welsh Walls.

A football team at Albert Road School with the headmaster, Mr Edwin Compton.

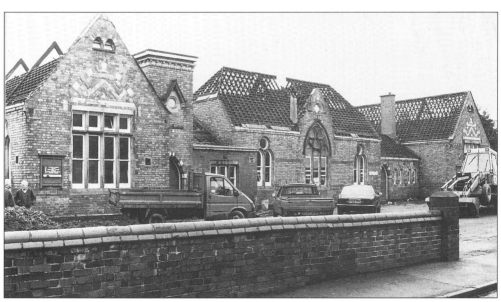

The sad demise of Albert Road School.

Seion Welsh Chapel Sunday school, 1909.

Horeb Welsh Chapel Sunday school concert in 1927.

A Hermon Chapel Literary Society social evening.

Chapel Street sisterhood glee club.

Willow Street in 1932.

The scene in Willow Street looking towards the Cross.

E.H. Longney's garage in Bailey Street. Now the premises of Bowen, Son and Watson, estate agents.

Markey, Taylor & Co were stamp distributors before the opening of the Post Office.

Shops to let at the corner of Willow Street and New Street.

H.E. Jordan, bootmaker and cobbler of Willow Street.

A view of Salop Road showing the Baptist Church and the spire of the Holy Trinity.

Remembrance Day, 1938.

The Queen's Hotel and Leg Street's celebrations for Queen Victoria's Diamond Jubilee in 1897.

The Mayoral Sunday procession to St Oswald's parish church (1960).

Church Street in its heyday and Cae Glas park resplendent with trees.

Castle Bank, believed to be glacial debris, first mentioned in a French novel of 1068.

The New Guildhall, Bailey Head, whose foundation stone was laid in 1892. It replaced the old Guildhall which was built in 1782 on the site of the Wool Hall. On the right is the Bailey Head pump which was installed in 1776 and removed by the council in 1958 to provide an extra car parking space.

The Red Lion Inn, Bailey Head was first noted in 1668. The Welsh Congregationalists held services in a room above the kitchen from 1840 to 1843.

A Victorian scene at the Bailey Head market with the original Powis Hall which was first mentioned in 1440 and became the Corn Exchange in 1838.

E.C. Hollywell's shop in Beatrice Street.

The Mechanics Arms, demolished during the redevelopment around Gate Street.

J.R. Jones, gentlemen's outfitters of London House, Willow Street.

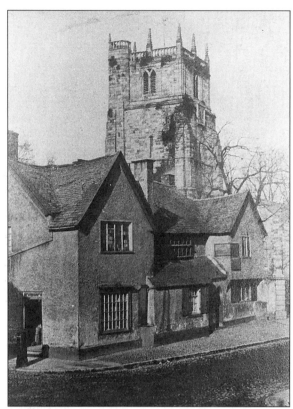

The Coach and Dogs, Church Street, pictured in 1863, was built by Edward Lloyd of Llanforda who rode in a dog carriage.

Pictured during demolition are the cottages that stood on the corner of Roft Street and Lower Brook Street, which were built in 1860. In the background is E.J. Gittins garage before modernisation.

Sergeant Witfield VC at the opening of Cae Glas Park.

An early line-up of Oswestry Constabulary at the Bailey Head. Note the 'sleeping policemen'!

The late Morgan Evans, auctioneer, at work with Vernon Carter at the re-opening of the Smithfield in 1961.

Doug Brereton auctions cattle in the ring in the attested section of the Oswestry Smithfield.

Sheep pens at the old Smithfield.

The Smithfield Market viewed from English Walls, built on Cae Tomley in 1849.

The Royal Hotel, Church Street, which later became E.J. Gittins cycle store, also housed Oswestry's first telephone exchange.

Regulars and staff outside the 'top' White Lion Inn, Willow Street.

Four generations of the family of J.E. Thomas photographed in the backyard of Joe Thomas' home in Roft Street.

Oswestry coopers demonstrate their barrels and churns.

The Oswestry division of the Royal Observer Corps at Shelf Bank in 1945.

WRAC's at Park Hall.

A group of Oswestry air-raid wardens.

Street celebrations at the end of the Second World War.

Plas Ffynnon in Middleton Road, which was acquired in the late 1850s by Thomas Savin, railway developer and Mayor in 1863.

A coach arriving at Plas Ffynnon, now the offices of the Inland Revenue.

Morda Road and the Gatehouse.

The Cross with the cast-iron lamp erected in 1862.

Staff at the rear of the Bear Hotel.

A vista across the Smithfield showing the smoking chimneys of the Dorset Owen Brewery and the locomotive works in the distance.

The original Barclays Bank in Cross Street.

Customers at the new cafeteria at Littlewoods store.

The Ropewalk during demolition.

Looking across Plough Bank prior to redevelopment.

Looking into Bailey Street from the site of the Osborne Hotel, now Poundstretchers.

Rubble being tipped at Swan Crescent during rebuilding.

The editorial staff of the *Border Counties Advertizer* outside Caxton Press in Oswald Road.

Cleaning the windows at Oswestry Station.

Two

Industry and Transport

The Locomotive Works photographed from Shelf Bank; the works were built by the Cambrian Railway Company 1865–1866 and were acquired by GWR in 1922 and closed by British Rail on 31 December 1966.

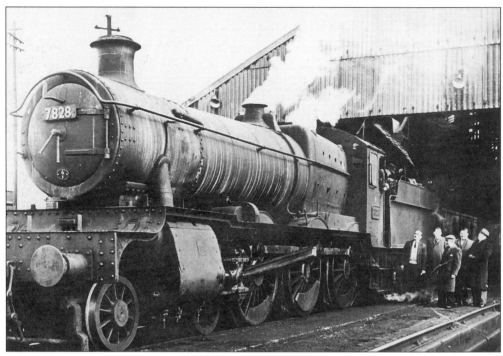

Odney Manor, the last steam train to leave Oswestry Locomotive Works in the 1960s.

Workmen at Cambrian Locomotive Works.

Oswestry railwaymen pictured on their annual trip to Blackpool in 1947.

The north end of Oswestry Railway Station. In the background is the goods depot, formerly the GWR passenger station.

Mr F.S. Roberts, the last manager of the
railway works, pictured on a Cambrian
engine.

The machine shop at Cambrian Railway Works.

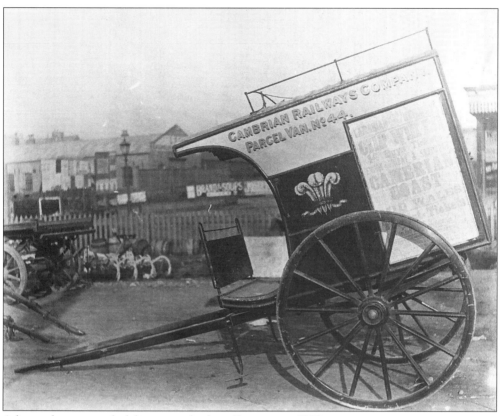

A horse-drawn parcels delivery van built at Oswestry in 1902.

The interior of Oswestry Carriage Works, including a horse-drawn carriage.

Oswestry's most serious rail accident. Firemen search the wreckage at the Baschurch crash, 13 February 1961.

Nantmawr junction: the crash of 7 August 1908.

The signalling staff at Kinnerley signal box.

The train at Kinnerley Station.

The crew of the No. 193 special.

The last day of the Shropshire and Montgomery Light Railway as pictured by *Advertizer* photographer Neville Pratt. The line ran from Shrewsbury to Llanymynech and was used to service the military depots.

A bus belonging to A. Hughes of Llansilin pictured in Willow Street. The Hughes brothers retired in the 1970s.

A Parish's of Morda coach at Oswestry Station on the local service to Crickheath.

J.E. Thomas & Sons, removers, at their Roft Street depot, now Regent's Court.

A Bedford lorry owned by Richard Burbidge's of Oswestry with driver John Oliver.

British Road Services with a wide load at Insulation Equipments.

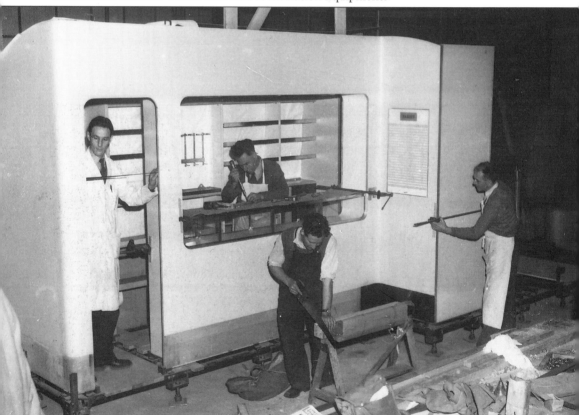

A British Rail buffet car under construction at Insulation Equipments (the 'plastics factory').

Jones & Co., corn merchants of England Walls, now the site of Kwik Save supermarket.

Workers at Jones & Co. with a loaded Scammell truck.

The West Midlands Gas Board first aid team.

A group of workers at Oswestry Gasworks.

Fitters outside the works of Edward Thomas', Farm Machinery of Whittington Road. Latterly it has been Frederick Jones & Son.

Employees of Jones & Evans, builders, of Oswestry, at Llangollen School.

Ifton 'B' Colliery first aid team.

J.R. Bartley's of Selattyn bus waiting outside the pithead baths at Ifton Colliery.

A general view of the Ifton Pit during its heydey.

Ifton pit with the locomotive *Unity* on the way to Preesgweene (Weston Rhyn) before the pit's closure in 1968.

Park Hall Halt, built to serve the Orthopaedic Hospital in the 1920s, with the Gobowen train leaving for Oswestry.

A coach party at the Greyhound Inn, Willow Street, which was rebuilt by Mr R.B. Smale.

Construction workers on the filter beds at Llanforda waterworks in the 1930s.

Bakers and delivery men with horse-drawn vehicles at Weston Bakery.

Oswestry High School junior drivers learn to reverse.

Shropshire Police demonstrate a patrol car at Oswestry Boys' High School.

Three

The Outskirts

Two local characters from Pant.

The Bebbington family at Rock House, Sweeney Mountain, c. 1905.

Will Kynaston, pig dealer of Pant, standing at the doorway of the Bradford Arms, Llanymynech, with his beloved pony, Dolly.

Offa Field Club at Nesscliffe Hill in 1922.

Colonel Campbell VC and the Tanatside harriers.

Brogyntyn Hall in past glory. The former home of Lord Harlech.

The Harlech family at home at Brogyntyn.

80

Members of Porthywaen Silver Band in 1934.

The Navigation Inn at Maesbury Wharf, Montgomery Canal.

A view of Oswestry Racecourse seen through the grandstand ruins, *c.* 1950.

Steam threshing at Perry Farm, Whittington, in 1935.

Workers at A.R.C. Blodwell Quarry, 1954. The quarry closed in 1990.

Dame Agnes Hunt and Sir Robert Jones, founders of the Orthopaedic Hospital.

Fire almost destroyed the Orthopaedic Hospital in 1948.

Tea and biscuits at a blood donor session.

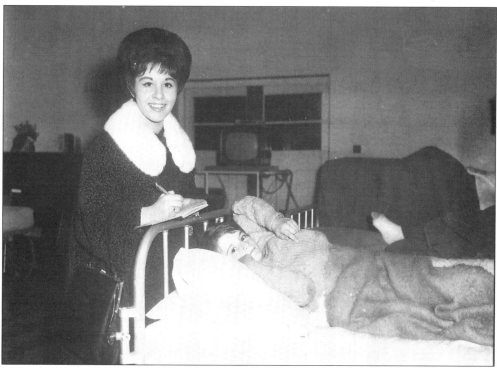

Helen Shapiro talking to Maureen Locke on a visit to the Orthopaedic Hospital.

The Junior Leaders Scottish Dance Team at Park Hall during the visit of Field Marshall Montgomery.

Crowds watching the display during Field Marshal Montgomery's visit to Park Hall Camp.

A rare view of the Garrison Theatre at Park Hall Camp before it was demolished.

The seventeenth TRRA inspection and march past at Park Hall in 1961.

A lesson in jam-making for girl members of Whittington and Oswestry Young Farmers' Club.

Whittington and Nescliffe Young Farmers' Club members at their ball in 1957.

Whittington and Oswestry Young Farmers' Club member Evan Hughes of St Martins competing in the world sheep-shearing championships, 1946.

Oswestry Show, 1962; judging the pigs.

The social scene at the Show, with the latest hats.

Oswestry Show, 1962; the Grand Parade.

The last meeting of Morda House Board of Guardians with members of Oswestry Incorporation, 17 March 1930. Morda House was built as a workhouse in 1791.

Four

Sport

The Trinity Guild football team of 1927.

Oswestry Town Football Club, 1928/9.

Oswestry Town Football Club, 1960.

George Antonio and Johnny Hancocks at a training sessions at Oswestry Football Club.

Oswestry Town players' training session at Victoria Road.

Roy Evans sets off along Willow Street in his Sunbeam Rapier for the Monte Carlo Rally.

Roy Evans ready to leave Willow Street for Glasgow in the Monte Carlo Rally.

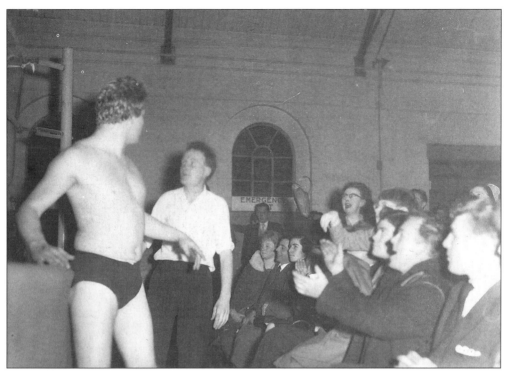

A fight outside the wrestling ring at the Old Baths.

Members of the Oswestry Paragon Cycle Club team leaving the Football Club in Victoria Road for a tour of the Briedden. In front are Malcolm Tudor and Mike Carter.

Oswestry Post Office bowls final at the Church Club.

Competitors at the Oswestry Boys Golf Championships.

Cambrian Juniors Football Club, 1906.

Bowlers at the Wynnstay, Oswestry's oldest green, first mentioned in 1769.

Mr Wynn Nicholls and greyhounds at Brogyntyn Gates.

The darts team of the Cross Foxes, Gobowen, 1930.

Five

The 1950s and 1960s

Mrs Davies modelling the latest fashions in town.

Rock 'n' Rollers at the opening of St Martins Youth Club at Rhyn Park School.

The Mayor's Ball, 1961.

Award winners at the Jack James School of Dancing at the Victoria Rooms.

Oswestry Rotary Club's party for senior citizens at the Drill Hall.

A St David's Day supper at Seion Welsh Chapel.

The Oswestry Chrysanthemum Society sale.

Mr J.E. Thomas, remover, handing over the bowling green in Cae Glas park to Oswestry Corporation.

A class for mentally disabled children at the clinic in Upper Brook Street.

The platform party at a Liberal Party fete in Cae Glas Park.

The 'Happy Go Lucky' skiffle group at Holy Trinity Church social evening.

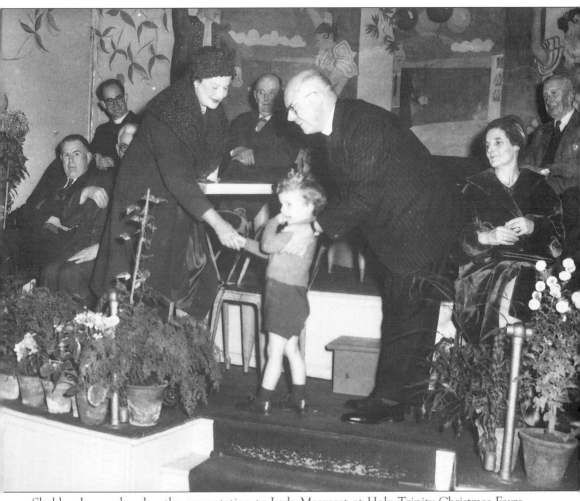

Sheldon Leonard makes the presentation to Lady Margaret at Holy Trinity Christmas Fayre.
After his tragic death in 1976, the Sheldon Leonard Memorial Charity was formed.

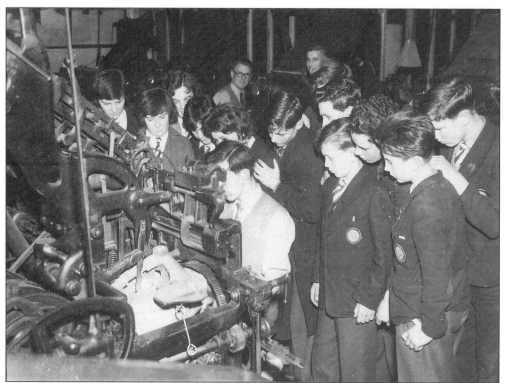

Pupils of St Martins School examine a linotype machine at Caxton Press, Oswestry, formerly the home of North Wales Newspapers.

1st Company, Oswestry Boys' Brigade visit the works at Caxton Press, Oswald Road.

Oswestry Boys' High School Speech Day, 1961.

An infants' class at Bellan House School.

Bellan House School playing fields.

Oswestry Girls' High School folk party, 1960.

Three pupils of Oswestry Girls' High School model the new school hats.

Dr Barnado's children's party at Oswald Road Chapel schoolroom.

MANWEB children's party at the Masonic Hall.

High summer in Cae Glas park; a family picnic.

Middleton Road schoolchildren at their Christmas party.

The Middleton Road schoolchildren's party.

The Rt Hon. Jo Grimmons MP speaking to Liberals at the Plaza.

Artistes who took part in a social evening at Greenfields Hospital, Morda.

Customers and helpers at the Liberal Party Fayre cake stall.

Terry White and Suzanne Powell digging the footings for Carreg Llwyd Evangelical Church.

Salop Road Baptist Fayre, 1961.
Children at the bran tub.

Helpers at Salop Baptist Fayre, 1961.

Helpers at Woodside Townswomen's Guild Autumn Fair.

The Croesoswallt Townswomen's Guild at their party at Smart's Cafe.

Oswestry Road Safety Rally. Car number one leaving the Smithfield.

St Oswald's parish church choir, 1950.

A group from Albert Road chapel off to a rally in Bristol.

Oswestry Girls' and Boys' High Schools' Choir.

A party for senior citizens at the old Woodside School.

Inspectors and officers of the Shropshire Yeomanry at the Drill Hall.

A class at Woodside School in 1950.

Oswestry Caged Birds Society Show at the Plough Hotel.

Oswestry scouts off to camp at Oswestry Station.

A Victorian view of Church Street.